Football Files

STRIKER

Michael Hurley

Raintree is an imprint of Capstone Global Library Limited, a company incorporated in England and Wales having its registered office at 7 Pilgrim Street, London, EC4V 6LB – Registered company number: 6695582

First published in hardback in 2010
Paperback edition first published in 2011

Edited by Louise Galpine, Vaarunika Dharmapala, and John-Paul Wilkins
Designed by Philippa Jenkins
Original illustrations © Capstone Global Library Ltd 2010
Illustrated by KJA-artists.com
Picture research by Hannah Taylor
Originated by Capstone Global Library Ltd
Printed and bound in China by Leo Paper Products Ltd

ISBN 978 1 406216 42 4 (hardback)
14 13 12 11 10
10 9 8 7 6 5 4 3 2 1

ISBN 978 1406217 39 1 (paperback)
15 14 13 12 11
10 9 8 7 6 5 4 3 2 1

British Library Cataloguing in Publication Data
Hurley, Michael
Striker. -- (Football files)
796.3'3423-dc22
A full catalogue record for this book is available from the British Library.

Acknowledgements
We would like to thank the following for permission to reproduce photographs: Action Images pp. **7** (Reuters/Susana Vera), **11** (Sporting Pictures), **15** (Reuters/Ruben Sprich), **18** (Reuters/Albert Gea), **28** (Reuters/Mike Blake); Corbis pp. **20** (Liewig Media Sports/Christian Liewig), **22** (epa/Kim Ludbrook), **26** (Reuters/Scanpix/ Bjorn Lindgren); Getty Images pp. **10** (Popperfoto), **14** (Bongarts/Alexander Hassenstein), **16** (Shaun Botterill), **23** (Alex Livesey); © KPT Power Photos **background image**; Press Association pp. **5** (LANDOV/Robin Parker), **8** (AP Photo/Tim Hales), **12** (AP Photo/POLFOTO, Tariq Mikkel Khan), **19** (Ap Photo/David Ramos), **24** (AP Photo/Victor R. Caivano); Shutterstock **background image** (© Nikola I).

Cover photograph of Argentina's Lionel Messi in action during a 2010 FIFA World Cup South American qualifier against Ecuador, Atahualpa Stadium, Quito, Ecuador, 10 June 2009, reproduced with permission of Getty Images/LatinContent/Patricio Realpe.

We would like to thank Dr Sarah Schenker for her invaluable help in the preparation of this book.

Every effort has been made to contact copyright holders of material reproduced in this book. Any omissions will be rectified in subsequent printings if notice is given to the publisher.

Disclaimer
All the Internet addresses (URLs) given in this book were valid at the time of going to press. However, due to the dynamic nature of the Internet, some addresses may have changed, or sites may have changed or ceased to exist since publication. While the author and publisher regret any inconvenience this may cause readers, no responsibility for any such changes can be accepted by either the author or the publisher.

CONTENTS

Some words are shown in bold, **like this**. You can find out what they mean by looking in the glossary on page 30.

BEING A STRIKER

Football is the most popular sport in the world. It is played by men and women, boys and girls. Almost every country in the world has a **professional** football **league**, but people everywhere play the game for fun, exercise, and excitement. People play in stadiums, parks, on the street, and in back gardens. All you need is something to use as a ball and a few friends.

Organized football matches have two teams with eleven players on each side. Each team is made up of players who have different positions and roles on the pitch. A team will usually have two strikers. It is the striker's job to score goals. Strikers help their teammates by **closing down** the opposition when they have the ball. They also help defend **set pieces**, like **corners** and **free kicks**.

All strikers need to be able to shoot accurately. Being good at **dribbling**, passing, and **heading** is also important. Some strikers are quick players who can dribble the ball skilfully. Other strikers are tall and powerful. They can head the ball well. Often a team will have a shorter, fast striker working with a taller, strong striker.

Here, Robin van Persie is in action for Arsenal. He has got very good technique. He can shoot, dribble, and pass the ball well.

FERNANDO TORRES

Fernando Torres plays for Liverpool and Spain. He grew up in Madrid, the capital city of Spain. When he was 15 years old he signed his first **professional** contract with Atletico Madrid, his favourite team. Torres' talent as a striker was obvious from an early age. He was quick, skilful, and determined. He also scored lots of goals.

Playing for Atletico Madrid

In 2001 Torres played for Spain at the Under 16 European Championships. Soon afterwards, he made his **debut** for Atletico Madrid in the Spanish second division. One week later he scored in only his second ever match. He broke two records at once, becoming not only the youngest player Atletico had ever had, but also the youngest to ever score a goal for them.

In the following season Torres was a regular member of the Atletico team. He helped them to get promoted into Spain's top division. Torres was also part of the Spain team that won the European Under 19 European Championship. He ended the tournament as the top scorer and was named player of the tournament.

"El Niño"

Fernando Torres is often called "El Niño". This is Spanish for "the kid". It is common in Spain for young sport stars to be given this nickname. The golfer Sergio Garcia is also known as "El Niño".

Captain of Atletico

Atletico named Torres as their captain for the 2003/04 season. He broke yet another record by becoming the youngest captain in the club's history. This achievement was well deserved. Along with his **pace** and scoring ability, Torres was also a leader on the pitch. He scored 19 goals in 35 league matches in his first season as captain.

In the same season he made his debut for Spain. He was part of the Spain **squad** for Euro 2004 (the **UEFA** European Championships). However, he made only **substitute** appearances in Spain's first two matches of the tournament. Then in the quarter-finals Spain lost 1–0 to the hosts, Portugal.

Fernando Torres (front) avoids Espanyol's Alex Fernandez during a Spanish Primera Liga match in 2005.

Fernando Torres (right) scores a goal against Hull City during an English Premier League match in 2009.

Throughout the next two seasons Torres continued to score goals for Atletico. He was now thought to be one of the best young talents in football. Many teams were interested in buying him, but he stayed loyal to his local club. In 2006 he played in the World Cup for Spain. He scored three goals in his first two matches. France knocked Spain out of the tournament at the quarter-final stage.

Moving to Liverpool

In 2007 Torres transferred to Liverpool for around £20 million. Liverpool broke their transfer record to sign him. He immediately became a favourite with the fans by scoring in his home debut game. He showed everybody just how good he was by receiving a pass and **dribbling** the ball past a **defender**, before shooting from a difficult angle. Torres scored lots of goals in his first season for Liverpool. He scored goals with his right foot and his left foot and also with his head.

The winning goal

The highlight of Torres' career so far was the 2008 UEFA European Championships. Spain won the tournament and Torres scored the winning goal in the final. He showed his skill by dribbling the ball past a defender, then calmly shooting the ball into the goal.

SHIELDING

One of Fernando Torres' most useful skills is his ability to shield the ball from an **opponent**. He uses his strength to back into a defender. He then gets safely past the defender whilst keeping the ball. At this point, he may choose to pass to a teammate.

1. A player receives a pass. She sees an opponent approaching.

2. The player shields the ball by positioning herself between it and her opponent.

3. The player must keep control of the ball, as well as avoid pushing or **fouling** her opponent. She passes the ball to a teammate.

PELÉ

Edison Arantes do Nascimento, better known as Pelé, is probably the greatest striker in history. Pelé began playing football as a child, on the streets of his home town in Brazil. When he was 11 years old Pelé's talent was noticed by a former Brazil footballer. He convinced Pelé's parents that Pelé had a bright future as a **professional** footballer. Pelé's father had also been a footballer. He let Pelé move to Brazil's largest city, São Paolo, to join the club Santos.

Pelé made his **debut** for Santos when he was only 15 years old and scored in that match. His long career with the club was just beginning. He stayed loyal to Santos throughout his career, although many big European clubs tried to sign him.

Pelé shoots as he is challenged by a Swedish defender in the 1958 World Cup final.

A star player

Pelé became famous all over the world for his incredible talent. When he was only 17 years old he was included in the **squad** for the 1958 World Cup. Pelé scored six goals in his first World Cup, including two in the final. Brazil beat Sweden 5–2. Football fans were amazed by the strength and skill of such a young player. He seemed to be able to do everything that a top footballer needs to do. His ball control was amazing. He had very good balance, which meant that he could **dribble** the ball past **opponents** easily. He could pass accurately and he could shoot powerfully with both his right and left foot.

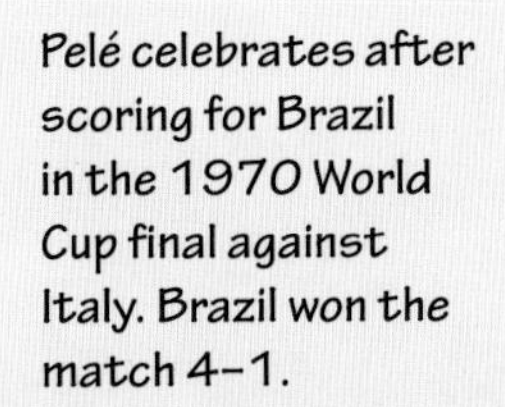

Pelé celebrates after scoring for Brazil in the 1970 World Cup final against Italy. Brazil won the match 4–1.

Injuries

Pelé played at another three World Cups for Brazil. In 1962 he was injured in the second match and had to watch as his teammates retained the title without him. Pelé was injured again at the 1966 World Cup. He was such a good player that the only way his opponents could stop him was to **foul** him. He often received injuries this way. Brazil did not win the World Cup in 1966.

However, Pelé helped Brazil to win the World Cup again in 1970. Brazil had an excellent team for the tournament, full of talented players. Pelé helped his team to the final with some outstanding performances and goals. In the final itself he scored for Brazil with a header.

Pelé played for Brazil 91 times and scored 77 goals, an incredible achievement. Pelé tried to retire in 1974, but he soon returned to the game to play football in the United States. He played for New York Cosmos for three years. By the time he finally retired in 1977, he had played over 1,300 matches and scored over 1,200 goals.

The greatest sportsmen

In 1999 Pelé was named second in a poll to find the greatest sportsman of the century. The former world heavyweight boxing champion, Muhammad Ali, was in first place.

Since retiring from football in 1977, Pelé has been involved in a lot of charity work. He has worked for **FIFA** as an ambassador and was also the Brazilian minister for sport in the 1990s.

HEADERS

Pelé scored in the World Cup final in 1970 with an unforgettable header. Try out the technique below. See how powerfully you can head the ball.

1.The ball is travelling through the air towards the player. He keeps his eyes on the ball, and pulls his shoulders and head back.

2. He pushes his head forwards to make contact with the ball, sending it flying.

Role models in football

Pelé visited Nigeria, Africa, to help promote Brazil's bid to host the Olympics in 2016. Brazil was successful in its bid and the host city will be Rio de Janeiro. Pelé met with 50 school children aged between 5 and 14 years old. He spoke to the children about sport and how important it can be in their lives. He also talked about the values that can be found in sport, such as respect and friendship.

Pelé was being a good role model to the children he met. This means he was showing them how they could improve their lives by acting as he did. To be a good footballer Pelé took care of himself by eating well and exercising. He also played the game fairly, showing respect to his teammates and opponents. These are good values for us all to share.

THIERRY HENRY

Thierry Henry has won the **league** title in three different countries. He has also won the World Cup with France and the **UEFA** European Championships. He has played football at the highest level since he was 17 and is still winning trophies.

Henry was born in France and moved to Monaco when he was 13 years old. He made his **debut** for Monaco in 1994. Henry won the French Young Player of the Year Award in 1996, and the following season he helped his team to win the league. He scored 9 goals in 36 matches. Henry left Monaco after 105 league appearances and 20 goals. In 1999 he joined Juventus, in Italy, for £10.5 million, but did not stay there for long. Henry's former manager at Monaco, Arsène Wenger, was now at Arsenal. He signed Henry from Juventus in the summer of 1999.

Here, Thierry Henry is in action for Monaco in 1996.

Playing for Arsenal

Henry's Arsenal career started slowly. He played eight games before he scored his first goal. His second season at Arsenal was much better and he scored 22 goals. He was soon known as one of the most feared strikers in the world.

The 2001/02 season was the best yet for Henry. He scored 31 goals to help his team win the league and the FA Cup. The next season Henry helped Arsenal win the FA Cup again and received the Professional Footballer's Association Player of the Year Award. He was the runner-up in the European and World Footballer of the Year Awards. He came second again for the same awards in the following season.

Thierry Henry receives his second place World Footballer of the Year Award in 2003.

Moving to Barcelona

In 2006 Arsenal made it to the final of the Champions League for the first time ever, but lost to Barcelona in the final. Henry stayed with Arsenal for a year after this disappointment, but moved to Barcelona in 2007. His transfer fee was £16 million. Henry was desperate to win the Champions League. It was the only trophy he had not yet won. However, after a difficult first season, he helped Barcelona to win the league, the Spanish Cup, and the Champions League in 2009. It was an incredible achievement.

Playing for France

Henry's international career began whilst he was still at Monaco. He made his debut for France before the 1998 World Cup. Henry was in the **squad** for the tournament and played in all of France's matches except the final. France won the final 3–0 against Brazil. Two years later France won the European Championships. Henry was in the squad and this time he played in the final. France won the final against Italy in extra time.

Thierry Henry won the Champions League with Barcelona in 2009. He finally got his hands on the one trophy he had not yet won.

Record breaker!

Thierry Henry holds the record for the highest number of goals scored in Arsenal's history. During his 8 seasons with the club he scored an amazing 226 goals.

DRIBBLING

Thierry Henry is well known for **dribbling** the ball along the left side of the pitch then shooting towards the far post of the goal. He can swerve the ball around the **goalkeeper** and into the goal. He has scored many times using this technique.

1.When running with the ball, the player pushes it forwards a short distance with the inside of her foot.

2. Using the outside of her foot this time, the player pushes the ball forwards again. By using the inside then the outside of her foot, the player can dribble the ball in a straight line.

France had an awful time at the 2002 World Cup, where they were knocked out at the group stage, and a disappointing Euro 2004, where they were beaten in the quarter-final. They returned to form by making it to the final of the 2006 World Cup. However, this time, it was Italy who beat France on penalties. They had their revenge for their 2000 defeat at France's hands!

Controversy

Henry caused controversy in 2009 when he handled the ball during a match for France against the Republic of Ireland. The hand ball led to a goal for France. The match was the second leg of a play-off to see who would make it to the 2010 World Cup. The referee did not see the incident and France won the match. Although Henry admitted to the hand ball after the match, **FIFA** decided that the result should stand.

LIONEL MESSI

Lionel Messi moved to Spain from his home town in Argentina when he was only 13 years old. The Barcelona team believed that young Messi would become a very special footballer one day. He is not very tall but he is quick and skilful. He can **dribble**, pass, and shoot accurately. He is a very unselfish player. This means that he often chooses to pass to a teammate who is in a better position to score, rather than try to take the glory for himself.

Multi-talented Messi

Messi is a striker, but because of his amazing skill he can play in many positions. He often begins matches playing on the right side of the pitch, but then moves into a more central position. It is very difficult for **defenders** to **mark** him. He has great balance and amazing dribbling ability. He can run with the ball and defenders cannot stop him without **fouling** him. In 2007 he scored a magnificent goal against Getafe in the Spanish Cup, the Copa del Ray. He dribbled the ball past four defenders and the **goalkeeper** before he shot into the goal. It was one of the greatest goals ever scored.

Lionel Messi has very good dribbling ability. He also has the strength to hold off defenders. Here, he is in action for Barcelona in a Spanish First Division match.

Playing for Barcelona

Messi made his league **debut** for Barcelona in 2004. He was only 17 years old. When Messi scored his first goal, he became the youngest ever goal-scorer in Barcelona history. In the summer of 2005 Messi represented Argentina in the Under 20 World Youth Championships. He finished the tournament as the top scorer with six goals, and was named player of the tournament. In the next season Messi became a regular for Barcelona. He made 17 appearances before an injury put him out of action for the rest of the season.

Lionel Messi (right) shoots past Atletico Madrid's goalkeeper to score a goal for Barcelona in 2009.

The best in the world

Messi has been compared with some of the greatest footballers in history. His Barcelona teammate Xavi Hernandez said, "I do not want to compare him to anyone, because whoever you compare him to will come off badly. Leo is by far the best in the world."

Messi is only 23 years old but he has already won many trophies in his career. He has won the Champions League, the Spanish Cup, and the Spanish **league** title three times. He was also part of the Argentina team that won gold at the 2008 Olympics. In recognition of these achievements, he was runner-up in the 2008 European and World Footballer of the Year Awards. In 2009, he won both these awards.

Disaster!

Lionel Messi made his debut for Argentina against Hungary in 2005. It was not the debut anyone had imagined it would be. It was a disaster. Messi lasted only 40 seconds on the pitch. He was sent off by the referee for elbowing an **opponent**.

Lionel Messi (centre) runs with the ball in a 2009 international friendly match between Argentina and France.

DRIBBLING AND CHANGING DIRECTION

When he is dribbling the ball, Lionel Messi is able to change direction very quickly. This makes it very difficult for opposition players to **tackle** him.

1.The attacker (in blue) is dribbling the ball. He is closely watched by the defender (in red) who is closing in.

2. As the defender closes in, he tries to tackle the attacker.

3. The attacker changes direction quickly and is able to run off with the ball. The defender has missed his chance to get possession of the ball.

Growing up

When Lionel Messi was a child, he was told by doctors that he had a growth hormone deficiency. This meant that he might not grow taller. His family could not afford to keep paying for the medicines that would help him. When he joined Barcelona, the club paid for his treatment.

KAKA

Ricardo Izecson dos Santos Leite is known to football fans all over the world as Kaka. He was born in Brasília, the capital city of Brazil. He moved to São Paulo when he was seven years old to join the football academy there. Kaka had a lot of ability and he trained every day. When he was just 15 years old he signed a **professional** contract with São Paulo.

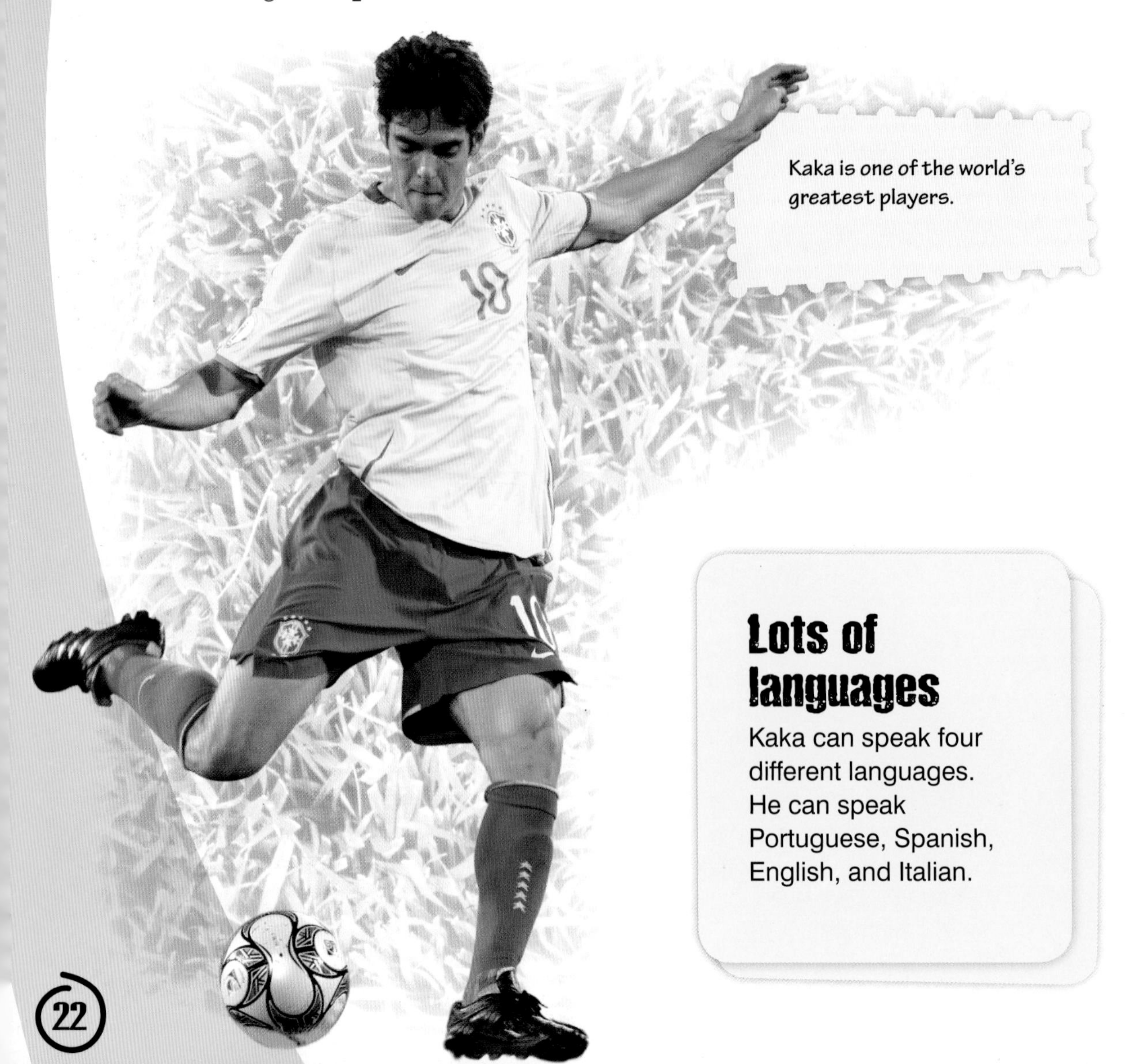

Kaka is one of the world's greatest players.

Lots of languages

Kaka can speak four different languages. He can speak Portuguese, Spanish, English, and Italian.

Serious injury

Kaka's football career nearly ended before it began. When he was 18 he hurt his back after a fall near a swimming pool. He was in a lot of pain and his doctors were afraid that he may have seriously damaged his back. Kaka was worried that he might not be able to play football again. Luckily, he made a full recovery.

Playing for São Paulo and AC Milan

Kaka scored two goals on his **debut** for São Paulo. He went on to play 58 times and to score 23 goals for the team before he was signed by AC Milan in 2003. There was a lot of interest in him from the big European clubs and São Paulo received a fee of £6 million from AC Milan. Kaka's first season with the team ended with them winning the **league** title. Kaka played as an attacking midfielder in his first season with AC Milan, but soon began playing as a striker.

Kaka is an intelligent player who can link the play between the midfield and the strikers. When he receives the ball from a teammate he can **dribble** it forward and shoot at the goal or he can choose to pass to another teammate. Kaka has very good technique and it is difficult for **defenders** to **tackle** him when he is running with the ball.

Kaka (standing) dribbles the ball past an opponent in the Champions League final in 2007.

AC Milan and beyond

In 2005 AC Milan reached the Champions League final. Kaka and his teammates had a very good first half and were 3–0 up at half-time, against Liverpool. In the second half Liverpool managed to score three goals to draw level, then AC Milan lost the match on **penalties**.

Two years later AC Milan and Liverpool were in the final again. Kaka had been the most important player for AC Milan during the tournament, scoring 10 goals. AC Milan went on to win the final 2–1. Kaka did not score, but he created one of the goals. After his amazing performances during the season, Kaka was named the 2007 **FIFA** World Player of the Year. After two more years with AC Milan Kaka transferred to Real Madrid. He signed to the club for around £55 million in the summer of 2009.

Kaka, standing beside Real Madrid legend Alfredo di Stéfano, displays his new kit to fans after his transfer from AC Milan in 2009.

Health and fitness

When Kaka was 17 he was skinny and had little physical strength. With the help of a specialized dietary and training regime, including swimming, he managed to gain around 16 kilograms of muscle.

VOLLEYS

When attempting a **volley** (strike a ball that is travelling through the air), Kaka knows that it is important to make the correct body shape. He needs to stay balanced when he strikes the ball.

1.To make a front-on volley, the player lifts his knee as the ball approaches, then swings his leg with his toes pointing down.

2. He makes contact with the ball against the front of his foot, keeping his head positioned above the ball.

TIPS FOR STRIKERS

Shooting

Strikers are expected to score goals so it is important that they can shoot the ball accurately. When you practise your shooting try running up to the ball and striking it with the top of your foot, against the laces of your trainers or boots. This will help the ball move in a straight line. Make sure that you have your head over the ball when you strike it. If you do not, the ball will probably go higher than you expected.

Italy's Mario Balotelli kicks a ball during a training session.

Dribbling

Not all strikers are good at **dribbling**, but it is a very helpful technique on the pitch. If you can dribble the ball you can get into goal-scoring positions or force the opposition players to **foul** you. If you are fouled your team will get a **free kick** or a **penalty**. Practise running with the ball at your feet. Try dribbling in a straight line, then try dribbling and changing direction. Finally, see if you can dribble the ball into a good goal-scoring position.

Short-range passing

All strikers must be able to pass accurately. Passing over a short distance to a teammate means that your team is more likely to keep possession of the ball. When passing over a short distance, keep your eyes on the ball and decide which direction you want the ball to go in. You must be able to judge the strength of your pass so that it reaches your teammate.

Heading

Accurate **heading** is a very useful skill for strikers to develop. At first, accuracy is more important than power when you are heading the ball. Once you have mastered your aim you can then try to increase the power of your headers. The power comes from your neck muscles. The more you practise, the stronger your neck muscles will become. When heading, remember to keep your eyes on the ball and try to time your jump so that your forehead makes contact with the ball at the peak of the jump.

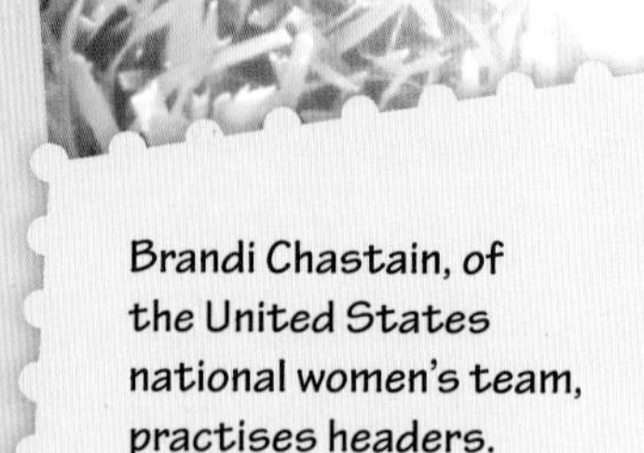

Brandi Chastain, of the United States national women's team, practises headers.

Volleys

Volleying the ball is one of the hardest skills to learn. A volley is when you kick the ball while it is in the air. It is important that you time your volley well. You must keep your eyes on the ball and **anticipate** when it will be in the right position for you to volley it. Practise kicking the ball when it is in the air and try to control the power of your kick. The more times you practise volleying the ball the easier it will become.

Penalties

Strikers are expected to score most of their team's goals. Sometimes they are expected to score from **penalties**. Accuracy is very important when you are taking a penalty. The most successful penalty-takers place their shots into the top corner of the goal, to make it impossible for the **goalkeeper** to save it. Some penalty-takers prefer to blast the ball as hard as they can. Try using the two different techniques and see how many times you can beat the goalkeeper.

GLOSSARY

anticipate perform before another player has a chance to react

closing down rushing the opposition to deny them space from which to attack

corner kick taken by the attacking team from the corner of the pitch after the defending team has knocked the ball over the goal line

debut first time a footballer plays for his team

defender position of a footballer on the pitch. Defenders try to stop the opposition from scoring.

dribble run with the ball

FIFA (*Fédération Internationale de Football Association*) the international organization responsible for football around the world

foul when a player breaks one of the rules of football. A foul could be a mis-timed tackle or a deliberate trip.

free kick kick of the ball awarded by the referee after a foul

goalkeeper position of a footballer on the pitch. The goalkeeper guards the goal and is the only player allowed to touch the ball with his hands.

header when you connect with the ball using your head

league group of teams that play against each other during the football season. There are national football leagues all over the world.

mark keep close to an opponent to try to stop them getting the ball

opponent/opposition person or team that you are playing against

pace speed. A player with lots of pace can move around the pitch quickly.

penalty the referee gives a penalty if a foul happens in the 18-yard box. The ball is placed on a spot 12 yards (10.9 metres) from the goal and only the goalkeeper is allowed to stop the shot.

professional being paid to do something. Professional footballers earn a salary for playing football.

set pieces when the ball is delivered from a standing position after a pause in play. Free kicks and corners are set pieces.

squad group of players from which a team is chosen. A squad is usually made up of around 20–25 players from which a team of 11 is chosen.

substitute player who does not start a match but who can replace a player on the pitch. Three substitutes can be used in most matches.

tackle take the ball from an opponent using your feet

UEFA (Union of European Football Associations) organization responsible for European football

volley when you kick a ball that is in the air

FIND OUT MORE

Books to read

Essential Sports: Football, Andy Smith (Heinemann Library, 2008)

Pelé (DK Biography), James Buckley (DK Publishing, 2007)

Skills (Know the Game): Soccer – Attacking (A&C Black, 2007)

Sport Files: Wayne Rooney, John Townsend (Raintree, 2009)

The World Cup series, Michael Hurley (Heinemann Library, 2009)

Usborne Activities: 50 Soccer Skills, Jonathan Sheikh-Miller (Usborne, 2008)

Websites

http://www.thefa.com/skills
The website of the English Football Association. This site has lots of videos to help you improve your skills and technique.

http://news.bbc.co.uk/sport2/hi/academy/default.stm
The BBC Sport Academy website includes videos and tutorials to help you learn more about playing football.

http://www.fifa.com/aboutfifa/developing/medical/playerhealth.html
The FIFA website has information about how to get the most out of playing football by eating healthily and avoiding injuries.

INDEX